*W*ithin you is an ideal,
a voice of youth,
and a promise of achievement
still to come.
Within your hands
are special gifts and talents.
Within your mind is the
source of your dreams...
Within you is the promise
of the future,
and I believe in you.

— Jean Lamey

THOUGHTS TO SHARE
WITH A WONDERFUL

TEENAGER

A BLUE MOUNTAIN ARTS®
COLLECTION

Blue Mountain Press®

SPS Studios, Inc., Boulder, Colorado

Library of Congress Catalog Card Number: 00-035243
ISBN: 0-88396-560-7

ACKNOWLEDGMENTS appear on page 64.

Poems by Susan Polis Schutz appearing in this publication: Copyright © 1972, 1974, 1978 Continental Publications; Copyright © 1983, 1984, 1997, 2000 Stephen Schutz and Susan Polis Schutz.

 Registered in the U.S. Patent and Trademark Office.
Certain trademarks are used under license.

Manufactured in the United States of America
First Printing: July 2000

This book is printed on recycled paper.

Library of Congress Cataloging-in-Publication Data

Thoughts to share with a wonderful teenager : a Blue Mountain Arts collection
    p. cm.
  ISBN 0-88396-560-7 (alk. paper)
    1. Conduct of life—Quotations, maxims, etc. 2. Conduct of life—Poetry. 3.
Adolescence—Quotations, maxims, etc. 4. Adolescence—Poetry. I. SPS Studios.

PN6084.C556 T497   2000
082—dc21   00-035243

SPS Studios, Inc.

P.O. Box 4549, Boulder, Colorado 80306

Contents

(Authors listed in order of first appearance)

Jean Lamey

Douglas Pagels

Toni Crossgrove Shippen

Leo Buscaglia

William Shakespeare

Susan Polis Schutz

Jacqueline Schiff

Socrates

Kahlil Gibran

Ralph Waldo Emerson

Christopher Morley

Somerset Maugham

Joseph Addison

Helen Keller

Henry van Dyke

Louise L. Hay

Judy LeSage

Ashley Rice

Barbara Cage

Allison Alexander

Mary A. Rothman

Ben Daniels

Donna Fargo

Deanna Beisser

Joanna Liese Wentz

Nancye Sims

Gael Henderson

Dolores Y. Patton

Linda Hersey

Collin McCarty

Edmund O'Neill

John Lubbock

Ben Jonson

Robert Louis Stevenson

Laura V. Nicholson

Kelly D. Caron

Millie P. Lorenz

Tara Knudson

Johann Wolfgang von Goethe

Anatole France

Berton Braley

Elisa Costanza

Marie Curie

Linda E. Knight

Henry David Thoreau

William Blake

Darwin P. Kingsley

Carson Wrenn

Susan Hickman Sater

Acknowledgments

"For My Teenager"
Words I Want You to Remember

I can barely begin to tell you of all my wishes for you • There are so many of them, and I want them all to come true • I want you to use your heart as a compass as you grow and find your way in the world, but I want you to always have an appreciation for the direction of home • I want you to be self-reliant, self-motivated, and self-sufficient, but to know that you will never be alone • I want you to be safe and smart and cautious • I want you to be wise beyond your years • I don't want you to grow up too fast • I want you to come to me with your fears •

For you, my teenager: I want the people who share your days to realize that they are in the presence of a very special someone ◆ You are a wonderful, rare person with no comparison ◆ I want you to know that opportunities will come, and you'll have many goals to achieve ◆ The more that obstacles get in the way of your dreams, the more you'll need to believe ◆ Get your feet wet with new experiences, but be sure you never get in over your head ◆ I want you to realize how capable you are, and that your possibilities are unlimited ◆ I hope you never lose your childlike wonder, your delight and appreciation in interesting things ◆ I know you'll keep responding in a positive way to the challenges life always brings ◆ I pray that you won't rush the future, and that you'll slowly build on the steppingstones of the past ◆ You have a strong foundation of family and friends and joy that will always last ◆

I wish I could find the words to tell you how much I love you each and every day ◆ But that feeling is so strong and its meaning is so magnificent, it can be hard to know just what to say ◆

I love you beyond all words ◆ And I promise that I will love you beyond all time ◆ So many treasures await you in your journey of life...

   and being blessed with you... has been mine ◆

— Douglas Pagels

In Case I Haven't Told You Lately...

I'm Proud of You, My Child

Many days go by
and I find myself saying
the same things to you
day in and day out:
"Clean your room."
"Is your room clean?"
"Do your homework."
"Did you finish your homework?"
"Don't be late."
"Take the trash out, please..."

Many nights, after you have
fallen asleep and look so peaceful,
I have wondered to myself...
Did I tell you that I love you?
That I appreciate all you do for me?
That through your entire life
you will find me in your cheering section?

Have I asked you lately
    about your happiness
and what's going on in your life?

I am sorry that there are so many times
when I get caught up with
the everyday routines
that I forget the simple,
important things in life.
I hope that you will forgive me
for my shortcomings,
as I will forgive you.
Always remember that
no matter how busy I seem to be,
I love you very much,
and I am proud of all that you do
and all that you stand for.

— Toni Crossgrove Shippen

A wonderful realization will be the day you realize that you are unique in all the world. There is nothing that is an accident. You are a special combination for a purpose — and don't let people tell you otherwise, even if they tell you that purpose is an illusion…. You are that combination so that you can do what is essential for you to do. Don't ever believe that you have nothing to contribute. The world is an incredible unfulfilled tapestry, and only you can fulfill the tiny space that is yours.

— Leo Buscaglia

Of all knowledge, the wise and good seek most to know themselves.

This above all: To thine own self be true.

— William Shakespeare

A Motto for Teenagers

Be an independent thinker
Make decisions
based on how you feel
and on what you know is right
regardless of what your peers
or other people think
Know yourself
Know what you can
and want to do in life,
Set goals
and work hard to achieve them
Have fun every day in every way
Be creative —
it is an expression of your feelings
Be sensitive in viewing the world
Trust in your family
Believe in love —
it is the most complete
and important emotion possible
Believe in yourself
and know that you are loved

— Susan Polis Schutz

Take These Thoughts with You on Your Journey Through Life

Don't ever forget that you are unique.
Be your best self
and not an imitation of someone else.
Find your strengths
and use them in a positive way.
Don't listen to those
who ridicule the choices you make.
Travel the road that you have chosen
and don't look back with regret.
You have to take chances
to make your dreams happen.
Remember that there is plenty of time
to travel another road — and still another —
in your journey through life.
Take the time to find the route
that is right for you.

You will learn something valuable
from every trip you take,
so don't be afraid to make mistakes.
Tell yourself that you're okay
just the way you are.
Make friends who respect your true self.
Take the time to be alone, too,
so you can know just how terrific
your own company can be.
Remember that being alone
doesn't always mean being lonely;
it can be a beautiful experience
of finding your creativity,
your heartfelt feelings,
and the calm and quiet peace deep inside you.

Please don't ever forget that you are special
and very much loved.

— Jacqueline Schiff

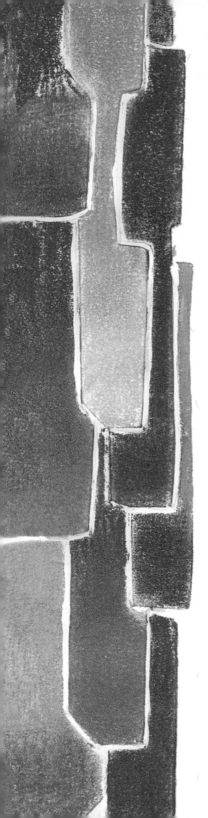

It is so important
to choose your own
lifestyle
and not let others
choose it for you

— Susan Polis Schutz

The greatest way to live with
honor in this world is to be
what we pretend to be.

— Socrates

You can walk freely
upon life's spacious path,
carpeted with flowers.
You are free to traverse the world,
making of your heart
a torch to light your way.
You can think, talk, and act freely;
you can write your name
on the face of life.

— Kahlil Gibran

Definition of a Successful Life

To laugh often and much;
to win the respect of intelligent people
and the affection of children;
to earn the appreciation of honest critics
and endure the betrayal of false friends;
to appreciate beauty, to find the best in others;
to leave the world a bit better,
whether by a healthy child,
a garden patch or a redeemed social condition;
to know even one life has breathed easier
because you have lived.

— Ralph Waldo Emerson

There is only one success — to be able
to spend your life in your own way.

— Christopher Morley

It's a funny thing about life;
if you refuse to accept
anything but the best,
you very often get it.

— Somerset Maugham

How To Be Happy...

———— ☆ ————

The grand essentials
to happiness
in this life are
something to do
something to love
and something
to hope for.

— Joseph Addison

Happiness cannot come from without. It must
come from within. It is not what we see and touch
or that which others do for us which makes us
happy; it is that which we think and feel and do,
first for the other fellow and then for ourselves.

— Helen Keller

Be glad of life
because it gives
you the chance
to love and to work
and to play and to
look up at the stars.

— Henry van Dyke

Find Happiness
in Everything You Do

Find happiness in nature
in the beauty of a mountain
in the serenity of the sea
Find happiness in friendship
in the fun of doing things together
in the sharing and understanding
Find happiness in your family
in the stability of knowing
    that someone cares
in the strength of love and honesty
Find happiness in yourself
in your mind and body
in your values and achievements
Find happiness in
everything
you
do

— Susan Polis Schutz

An Affirmation
for Teenagers

I communicate freely.

It is safe for me to grow up. I love
to learn and grow and change, and
I feel safe in the midst of it all,
knowing that change is a natural
part of life. My personality is
flexible, and it is easy for me to
go with the flow of life. My inner
being is consistent; therefore, I am
safe in every kind of experience.
When I was a little child, I did not
know what the future would bring.
As I now begin my journey into
adulthood, I realize that tomorrow
is equally unknown and mysterious.
I choose to believe that it is safe for
me to grow up and take charge of
my life. My first adult act is to
learn to love myself unconditionally,
for then I can handle whatever the
future may bring.

— Louise L. Hay

No Matter What Choices
You Make in Life,
You're Still a Part of Me

Your choices in life are so different from
   what I would have chosen for you
I dreamed so many dreams for you
I wanted your life to be perfect
And I guess I forgot whose life it was
I guess I forgot they were my dreams — not yours
You have learned so many things the hard way
But I guess that's the only way you knew how to learn
I want you to know that even though you've
   chosen your own path to follow
I will always be there to love and support you
I know I won't always agree with you
But I also know that I have to let you figure
   things out for yourself
It's hard for me to let go
And it's hard for me to let you make mistakes
But I know you are a strong and capable person
And in the end you will triumph
Because even though you are your own person
You're still a part of me

— Judy LeSage

Thoughts from the Heart
of a Teenager

Give us our little wishes, our own clothes, our harmless rebellions. The chance to make our own mistakes, to grow our special gardens. Tolerate our musings, as we learn and change our minds. Don't lead or we won't learn to walk alone, to see, or speak our minds.

Listen before you judge us; we feel deeply and have reasons, too. Remember we must chase different dreams before we find what we best can do.

Trust our actions and our choices,
however different from your own.
Give us the courage to take chances, to
know if we fall we are not alone. Have
patience with our yearnings as we see
our intentions through. Let us know that
where we are coming from is a safe place
to return to.

Allow us the freedom to be creative, the
opportunity to be wrong. Teach us that
we don't have to be perfect to belong.
Give us our secret plans, our own music,
our space to grow. Learn with us as we
discover these things. When the time is
right, let us go.

— Ashley Rice

What Is a Teenager?

A teenager is a person who is part child and part adult.

A teenager is someone who loves to have fun and thrives on excitement, yet sometimes feels overwhelmed by new responsibilities and expectations.

A teenager is someone who is still learning from the past and is unsure about the future.

A teenager is someone who craves friends and an active social life, yet finds that you can't please everyone.

A teenager is someone who needs someone in his or her life who is a good example, who can be trusted with secrets, who is an avid listener.

A teenager is someone who needs to know that life always gets better and that things worth having are worth working and waiting for.

A teenager is someone who needs to
    understand that trying, combined
    with persistence and determination,
    are the biggest parts of succeeding
    and that mistakes are okay as long as
    you learn from them.

In between the joy of being a protected,
    cherished child
and the contentment of being a free,
    independent adult
is the fun
the frustration
the confusion
the boredom
the excitement
the despondence
and the elation
of a
teenager.

— Barbara Cage

This isn't an easy world
    to be growing up in,
and I don't blame you
if you sometimes feel
a little confused about things.

For now, remember that it's
okay to feel the way you feel.
Be yourself, and don't try to
    hide what's going on inside.
Just don't forget
that a beautiful person lives there.

Even though you sometimes
    feel unhappy
with the way things are going,
    don't ever stay sad for long.

I miss you
when the happy you
        is gone.

And I'll always be here
to help you when
you need to find
    your smile again.

— Allison Alexander

Don't Let Things
Get You Down

Life can be unfair at times,
and those are the times
when you must maintain faith
and never let go.
It is especially during the difficult times
that you must live your life
to its fullest potential
and triumph over circumstances
with hope and courage.
Life isn't always easy,
but if you keep going and persevere
to the very best of your ability,
you will gain strength to manage
the new challenges ahead.
Each goal that you reach
is another important step forward.
Believe that there are
bright and wonderful days
ahead for you,
and you will find them.

— Mary A. Rothman

Even When Nothing
Feels Right in Your Life...

Refuse to be unhappy;
   be cheerful instead.
Refuse to let your troubles multiply;
   just take them one by one.
Organize your time; keep your life simple
   and exactly the way you want it.
Refuse to complain about things;
   learn to improve your surroundings
and create your world
   the way you believe it should be.
Refuse to dwell on the mistakes
   or disappointments
that are sometimes a part of life;
instead learn how you can
   make things better.
Be optimistic.
Be energetic and positive
   about the things you do,
and always hope for the best.
Believe in yourself at all times
   and in all aspects of your life.

— Ben Daniels

Do your best, my child, and realize that I love you

Sometimes you
think that you
need to be perfect
that you cannot
make mistakes
At these times
you put so much
pressure on yourself
I wish that you
would realize
that you are
a human being —
like everyone else
capable of
reaching great potential
but not capable of
being perfect
So please
just do your best
and realize that
this is enough
Don't compare yourself
to anyone
Be happy to be
the wonderful
unique, very special
person that you are

— Susan Polis Schutz

Accept Yourself

We need to accept ourselves, just as we accept the color of our eyes. They're either brown, blue, green, or some variation. One color is not better or worse. They are all beautiful, and we wouldn't try to change them.

Our personalities are developed from influences, such as family, society, schools, and church. We are the result of all that has collected on us to make us unique. Much like the color of our eyes, our ways are set. This doesn't mean we should not try to change something that we really want to change, but, rather, it is about using acceptance as a catalyst to make changes happen. If we're in a state of acceptance, there is more freedom of choice and, therefore, a better opportunity to succeed.

Ask yourself these questions: Is putting myself down getting the job done? Do I respond better to criticism or acceptance? Am I more motivated by turmoil or ease? Do I find it easier to do something if I <u>have to</u> or just <u>want to</u>? How long have I been trying to make this change using the same tactics I've been using?

Sometimes listening to your own answers is more helpful than "should have's" or "could have's." As you search to get along better in life and try to understand your own nature and resistance to change, maybe you need to hear more acceptance of yourself than reprimands.

Criticism often takes away the freedom to choose to do something. Acceptance helps us believe we can change or do something we want to. Sometimes we need to take off our running shoes and boxing gloves and stop the lectures and criticisms. We need approval and acceptance of our imperfections, the same kind of simple acceptance we have for the color of our eyes.

You're good, unique, and special.
Accept yourself!

— Donna Fargo

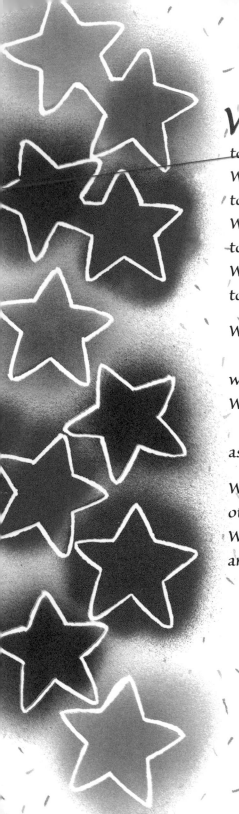

We need to feel more
to understand others
We need to love more
to be loved back
We need to cry more
to cleanse ourselves
We need to laugh more
to enjoy ourselves

We need to establish the values
    of honesty and fairness
when interacting with people
We need to establish a strong
    ethical basis
as a way of life

We need to see more
other than our own little fantasies
We need to hear more
and listen to the needs of others

We need to give more
and take less
We need to share more
and own less
We need to realize the importance of the family
as a backbone to stability
We need to look more
and realize that we are not so different from
   one another

We need to create a world where
we can all peacefully live
the life we choose
We need to create a world where
we can trust each other

— Susan Polis Schutz

Some Thoughts
About How to Resolve
Disagreements in Your Life

Whenever you become involved
in a confrontation,
it's best to allow yourself
some time to really think about
all sides of the situation.
Before becoming defensive,
give yourself the opportunity
    to be receptive.
Remember that all problems have
    more than one answer;
there are always
    extenuating circumstances
for everyone to consider.

Be willing to listen;
    be open to the possibility
that things can be worked out,
because you can reach a compromise
    out of any conclusion.
Before you enter into
    a major debate,
take time to compose
    your thoughts and feelings.
Realize that anything
    and everything in life
has its own unique perspective,
and before you jump
    to any conclusions,
it's important to allow yourself
the time to completely understand.

— Deanna Beisser

Remember that Good Sportsmanship Applies to All Aspects of Life

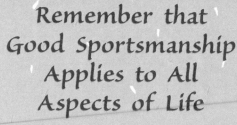

Good sportsmanship is more than
    shaking hands;
it's admitting you've been defeated
    even when you tried your best.
It's having enough courage to hand over
    the victory to your opponent
and congratulate him —
hoping that one day you, too, will be
    standing at the top of the podium.
Only then can you look back and say
    "It all paid off" —
hoping that you're not the only one
    with good sportsmanship.
For you see, good sportsmanship is
    more than shaking hands.
It's also a standard —
    a goal of self-worth.
It's having the heart to know that,
while you might not have reached
    your own goals,
you can rejoice in the fact that
    someone else did.

— Joanna Liese Wentz

Winners Are
People like You

Winners take chances.
Like everyone else, they fear failing,
but they refuse to let fear control them.
Winners don't give up.
When life gets rough, they hang in
until the going gets better.
Winners don't blame fate for their failures
nor luck for their successes.
Winners accept responsibility for their lives.
Winners are positive thinkers
who see good in all things.
From the ordinary, they make the extraordinary.
Winners believe in the path they have chosen
even when it's hard,
even when others can't see where they are going.
Winners are patient.
They know a goal is only as worthy
as the effort that's required to achieve it.
Winners are people like you.
They make this world a
better place to be.

— Nancye Sims

Don't Grow Up Too Fast

When we are young, we cannot wait to be older —
    to talk, to walk, to go to school,
    to drive, to date, to graduate,
    to fall in love, to get a job,
        to make our own lives.
But don't be in too much hurry to grow up.
When you are older, your childhood is the place
      you will go
    to reminisce, to find answers,
    to seek comfort, to reassure,
      to understand yourself.
It is a time that will shine in your mind and bring you
    thoughts of warmth, security, and love.
Many times, places, and people make the memories
      of childhood,
    and they become more precious the older you get.
      I can tell you this from experience —
    adulthood comes soon enough
      with its responsibilities and cares.
Don't hurry through this time —
    slow down, make the most of it,
      and savor the memories.

                — Gael Henderson

Memories of Your Teenage Years
Will Last Forever

Years will come and go in your life,
but it seems that your teenage years
are both the happiest
and saddest of them all.
You are happy you made it this far,
and you are sad that so many
of your carefree days are gone.
But the memories you have
can never be taken away:
memories of dances attended
and dances missed,
of that one and only person
you loved (and whose name you
forgot the following week),
of teachers who made
an impression on you
and whom you will remember
for the rest of your life,
and of all the people who have faith in you
to make it all the way through.

— Dolores Y. Patton

It seems fashionable these days
for everyone in a family to go
    their separate ways
and do their own things.
And while I appreciate that we
    all have our own schedules,
we are still part of a family.
We should work harder to stay close
and do things together —
like laughing, having fun,
and talking
whenever one of us has a problem.
Some people might think
that it's a little late
    for us to start doing this —
but I would like to think
that it's never too late
to reconnect with the people
you love most —
your family.

— Linda Hersey

A Family Is Love

Wherever we go
and whatever we do,
let us live with this
remembrance in our hearts...
that we are family.

What we give to one another
comes full circle.
May we always be
the best of friends;
may we always be one another's
rainbow on a cloudy day;
as we have been yesterday
and today to each other,
may we be so blessed
in all our tomorrows...
over and over again.

For we are a family,
and that means love
that has no end.

— Collin McCarty

Your Life Holds
Unlimited Potential
and Wonderful Dreams

You have the ability
to attain whatever you seek;
within you is every potential
you can imagine.
Always aim higher than
you believe you can reach.
So often, you'll discover
that when your talents
are set free
by your imagination,
you can achieve any goal.
If people offer
their help or wisdom
as you go through life,
accept it gratefully.
You can learn much from those
who have gone before you.

Never be afraid or hesitant
to step off the accepted path
and head in your own direction
if your heart tells you
that it's the right way for you.
Always believe that you will
ultimately succeed
at whatever you do,
and never forget the value
of persistence, discipline,
and determination.
You are meant to be
whatever you dream
of becoming.

— Edmund O'Neill

The Decisions You Make Today Influence All Your Tomorrows

I know that you crave fun and excitement, and that being with your friends and doing what they do is part of that fun.

But only you can decide whether the choices you make are going to be the best for you.

Though you may be tempted by a dare to prove yourself, always realize that you are the only one to whom you must prove yourself.

Realize that your body is precious, and it has to last you a lifetime. Don't do things that put it in danger or cause it unrepairable harm.

Your heart and conscience are your own, and you have to live with them. So don't do anything that hurts or shames another.

I believe that you know right from wrong, and I realize the temptations that come along.

I just hope and pray that you'll love yourself enough to resist when things are wrong and not in your best interest.

I have loved and protected you your whole life, and the hardest thing to do in the world is let you go — to trust you to love yourself as I have loved you and to take care of yourself as I would care for you.

Now you're the one responsible for the decisions you make and the future you'll have. I have always had your health and happiness, your present and future, at heart. I hope you'll do the same. I love you, my child, more than you will ever know.

— Barbara Cage

REMEMBER THE IMPORTANCE OF FRIENDSHIP

——————— ☆ ———————

The only way to have a friend is to be one.

— Ralph Waldo Emerson

Much certainty of the happiness and purity of our lives depends on our making a wise choice of our companions and friends.

— John Lubbock

True happiness consists not in the multitude of friends, but in their worth and choice.

— Ben Jonson

We are all travellers in the wilderness of this world, and the best that we find in our travels is an honest friend.

— Robert Louis Stevenson

There is no need for an outpouring
of words to explain oneself to a friend
Friends understand each other's thoughts
even before they are spoken

— Susan Polis Schutz

Some people will be your friend
because of whom you know
Some people will be your friend
because of your position
Some people will be your friend
because of the way you look
Some people will be your friend
because of your possessions
But the only real friends
are the people who will be your friends
because they like you for how you are inside

— Susan Polis Schutz

Be a Good Friend to Others

"Friend."
Some people take this word for granted.
They use it to describe almost anyone
who touches their lives.
But that's not fair,
for not everyone fits this word.
It is easy to be a pal, a buddy,
a companion, or an acquaintance,
but to be a friend means
so very much more.

To be a friend
means being trusted and trusting.
Honest and dedicated.
Supportive and available.
It means going strong with
your own life's work and plans,
yet reaching out to another when you're needed
(and maybe even when you're not).
To be a friend is to be fun and fair.
Serious and silly.
To make the mundane exciting.
The unexpected acceptable.
To be the silent stronghold without being asked.
To feel happy for someone else's happiness,
and to share the burden of sorrow
in thought and action.

To be a friend
is to be strong enough to be leaned on
when someone else cannot walk another step
and to look to that other person
for your own tranquility
when the world has spun you out of control.
It is a lot of giving, a lot of taking,
but most of all, a lot of sharing.

The qualifications of being a friend
are too high for the ordinary to reach.
It takes a while to earn the title
and a lifetime to truly know its meaning.
Never take the job lightly
or give it away too quickly;
it must be cultivated, nurtured, and cared for.
For when you truly find a "friend,"
you are lucky enough to have one for life.

— Laura V. Nicholson

Don't Walk Alone
Through Life

The world is too big a place
to walk through alone.
There are too many city streets
    and too many dirt roads.
There are too many hours
    to fill by yourself,
and too many empty moments.
There are too many lonely hearts
    that need to be loved,
too many strangers who need
    to be welcomed,
too many people who are in need
    and should be helped,
and too many things to share.

One person alone might take
   for granted something
that two or more people together
   learn to appreciate.
There are too many stars
   to count by yourself
and too many birds to feed.

If you walk alone,
who will be there to answer the phone
when you decide to call?
Who will grasp your hand
   when you reach out?
Who will pick up the pieces
   if your world were to fall apart?
Time is too short
to not reach out to others.
Don't walk alone.

— Kelly D. Caron

If I could bring you a world full of happiness, I would. If I could take your sadness and pain and feel them for you, I would. If I could give you the strength to handle the problems that this world may have for you, I'd do that, too. There is nothing that I wouldn't do for you to bring laughter instead of tears into your life.

I can't give you happiness, but I can feel it with you. I can't take away all your hurts in this world, but I can share them with you. I can't give you strength when you need it the most, but I can try to be strong for you.

I can be there to tell you how much I love you. In times when you feel you need to reach out to someone, I can be there for you, not to change how you feel, but to go through these times with you.

When you were little, I could hold you in my arms to comfort you, but you'll never be too grown up for me to put my arms around you. You are so very special to me, and the most precious gift I could have ever received was you on the day you were born. I love you!

— Millie P. Lorenz

You Are a
Wonderful Teenager

I have asked myself
    (as every parent does)
if I have loved you enough
and done the very best job
    that I could for you.
Then, as human nature goes,
    I remembered mistakes
        that I have made
and how they might have hurt you.
Yet I have never stopped loving you,
    even in the times when
        I seemed distant.

I am so proud that you are my child;
when I think of you,
    I feel tears in my eyes
because you make me so happy.
I wonder why I haven't told you this
    much more often than I have,
but sometimes it's hardest to say
    what we feel strongest about.
So I don't want to let
    another moment pass
without telling you
how much you mean to me
and how very much I love you.

— Linda Hersey

Wherever Your Destiny
Leads You...

May you learn along the way
about life, yourself,
and who you want to be.

You will meet many people.
May you treat each individual
with kindness and respect,
just as you want to be treated.

You will make new friends.
May you remember to keep in touch
with the old friends, too —
the ones who love you very much.

You will face many problems.
May you come to accept
that life is not easy.
Be strong, and do the best
that you can do.

You will make mistakes.
May you learn from them
so that you can grow
and move on as a stronger
and wiser person.

You will make important decisions.
May you know yourself
and choose what is best for you.
If you are confused,
just listen to your heart.

You will set goals for yourself.
May you have the courage
to make your dreams come true
and live the life that you want.

— Tara Knudson

REACH FOR YOUR DREAMS...

Whatever you can do or dream you can do, begin it. Boldness has genius and magic and power in it.

— Johann Wolfgang von Goethe

To accomplish great things, we must not only act but also dream, not only plan but also believe.

— Anatole France

Enthusiasm is one of the most powerful engines of success. When you do a thing, do it with all your might.... Be active, be energetic, be enthusiastic and faithful, and you will accomplish your objective.

— Ralph Waldo Emerson

If you want a thing bad enough
To go out and fight for it,
Work day and night for it,
Give up your time and your peace and your sleep for it,
If only desire of it
Makes you quite mad enough
Never to tire of it,
Makes you hold all other things tawdry and cheap for it,
If life seems all empty and useless without it
And all that you scheme and you dream is about it,
If gladly you'll sweat for it,
Fret for it,
Plan for it,
Lose all your terror of God or man for it,
If you'll simply go after that thing that you want,
With all your capacity,
Strength and sagacity,
Faith, hope and confidence, stern pertinacity,
If neither cold poverty, famished and gaunt,
Nor sickness nor pain
Of body or brain
Can turn you away from the thing that you want,
If dogged and grim you besiege and beset it,
   You'll get it!

                    — Berton Braley

Many people speak of dreams as fanciful things like fairies and charmed rings and lands of enchantment. Others only believe in faraway dreams such as stars or sea castles with elf-like inhabitants.

There are day-dreamers and night-dreamers who dream up make-believe places. They use much imagination, and in that are dream gifted. But the serious dreamers are those who catch dreams to bring them to life, and show that when they were dreaming, they meant it.

— Ashley Rice

Don't ever give up your dreams...
and never leave them behind.
Find them; make them yours,
and all through your life,
cherish them,
and never let them go.

— Elisa Costanza

To be what we are, and to become what we are capable of becoming is the only end of life.

— Robert Louis Stevenson

The future belongs to those who believe
in the beauty of their dreams.

— Marie Curie

Go forward with your dreams;
let their power lead you on.
Grow and learn as you go,
and never stop believing.
Move ahead with confidence,
always reaching forward.
The opportunities awaiting you are endless;
enjoy them as they unfold.
Find your place in the world,
and let your own star shine bright.
Never give up; always press on.
Each day is a fresh place to begin.
Get behind what you believe,
open your soul, and honor your dreams.
Celebrate who you are, all that you've done,
and all you've yet to accomplish.
Go for it!
May your future be bright
    with happiness and success.

— Linda E. Knight

LOOK TO THE FUTURE...

─────── ☆ ───────

If one advances confidently
in the direction of his dreams,
and endeavors to live
the life which he has imagined,
he will meet with
a success unexpected
in common hours.

— Henry David Thoreau

No bird soars too high,
if he soars with his own wings.

— William Blake

You have powers you never
dreamed of. You can do things
you never thought you could
do. There are no limitations in
what you can do except the
limitations in your own mind
as to what you cannot do.
Don't think you cannot.
Think you can.

— Darwin P. Kingsley

Be Happy, My Child

Chase your wishes and follow your dreams.
Carry the sun inside you.
Get a little closer, every single day,
    to the hopes that you want to come true.

Believe in tomorrow and stretch your wings.
Embrace your blessings and appreciate all
    the sweet memories you have made.
Reach for your stars, brighten your days.
Fill your heart in a thousand ways.

Be happy, my child.
I love you so much, and I wish you
    such wonderful things.
I wish you joys that only a dreamer
    would dream
and things that only a parent would wish for,
    and I pray…

    May you never forget
        that my heart and my hopes
            are with you each step of the way.

— Carson Wrenn

May All Your Dreams
Come True

Lean against a tree
and dream your world of dreams
Work hard at what you like to do
and try to overcome all obstacles
Laugh at your mistakes
and praise yourself for learning from them
As you go through life
pick some flowers
and appreciate the beauty of nature
Be honest with people
and enjoy the good in them

Don't be afraid to show your emotions
Laughing and crying make you feel better
Love your friends and family
    with your entire being
They are the most important part of your life
Feel the calmness on a quiet sunny day
and plan what you want to accomplish in life
Find a rainbow
and live your
world of dreams

— Susan Polis Schutz

To My Teenager

...As Long as We Remain Open with Each Other, We'll Grow Together

I know sometimes you think
   I don't understand you,
but I do remember how difficult
   being a teenager is.
I know it is not easy
   working through
all the feelings
   you are experiencing,
and I hope that you will always
   feel free
to turn to me about any subject.

Your teenage years should be filled
with wonderful experiences,
and I want all the times
   in your life
to be fulfilling and enjoyable!
I know sometimes you think
I am being too nosy about your
   private life
or I am telling you what to do,
but I am not trying to make you feel
   as if you have no independence.

I know you need your own space at times,
and I understand you need room to grow.
But as your parent, I want you to be healthy and happy
and have every opportunity in life you deserve.
When I put my foot down
or make a few rules for you to follow,
I'm doing what I think is best for you.

Still, I want us always to be able
to work through any of our differences
and communicate openly with each other.
Just as any relationship has its ups and downs,
so will ours as parent and child.
We have always had a good relationship,
and I think we can grow and learn together
in all the years ahead if we both work hard
at listening to and respecting each other.
You are very important to me.
I hope you know I love you with all my heart,
and I am proud to be your parent.

— Susan Hickman Sater

ACKNOWLEDGMENTS

We gratefully acknowledge the permission granted by the following authors, publishers, and authors' representatives to reprint poems or excerpts from their publications.

Leo F. Buscaglia, Inc. for "A wonderful realization..." from LIVING, LOVING & LEARNING by Leo Buscaglia, Ph.D., published by Ballantine Books. Copyright © 1982 by Leo F. Buscaglia, Inc. All rights reserved. Reprinted by permission.

Citadel Press, an imprint of Kensington Publishing, for "You can walk freely..." from A SECOND TREASURY OF KAHLIL GIBRAN by Kahlil Gibran, translated by Anthony Ferris. Copyright © 1962 by Citadel Press, an imprint of Kensington Publishing. All rights reserved. Reprinted by permission.

Judy LeSage for "No Matter What Choices You Make in Life, You're Still a Part of Me." Copyright © 1999 by Judy LeSage. All rights reserved. Reprinted by permission.

Hay House, Inc. for "I communicate freely." from MEDITATIONS TO HEAL YOUR LIFE by Louise L. Hay. Copyright © 1994 by Louise L. Hay. All rights reserved. Reprinted by permission of the publisher, Hay House, Inc., Carlsbad, CA.

Barbara Cage for "A teenager is a person who...." Copyright © 1999 by Barbara Cage. And for "The Decisions You Make Today Influence All Your Tomorrows." Copyright © 2000 by Barbara Cage. All rights reserved. Reprinted by permission.

PrimaDonna Entertainment Corp. for "Accept Yourself" by Donna Fargo. Copyright © 1999 by PrimaDonna Entertainment Corp. All rights reserved. Reprinted by permission.

Joanna Liese Wentz for "Remember that Good Sportsmanship Applies to All Aspects of Life." Copyright © 2000 by Joanna Liese Wentz. All rights reserved. Reprinted by permission.

Gael Henderson for "Don't Grow Up Too Fast." Copyright © 2000 by Gael Henderson. All rights reserved. Reprinted by permission.

Linda Hersey for "It seems fashionable these days...." Copyright © 2000 by Linda Hersey. All rights reserved. Reprinted by permission.

Kelly D. Caron for "Don't Walk Alone Through Life." Copyright © 1999 by Kelly D. Caron. All rights reserved. Reprinted by permission.

A careful effort has been made to trace the ownership of poems used in this anthology in order to obtain permission to reprint copyrighted materials and give proper credit to the copyright owners. If any error or omission has occurred, it is completely inadvertent, and we would like to make corrections in future editions provided that written notification is made to the publisher:

SPS STUDIOS, INC., P.O. Box 4549, Boulder, Colorado 80306.